The
New Read, Write
and Remember

BOOK
3

Constance Milburn

Nelson

numbers

1	one	5	five	9	nine
2	two	6	six	10	ten
3	three	7	seven	11	eleven
4	four	8	eight	12	twelve

colours

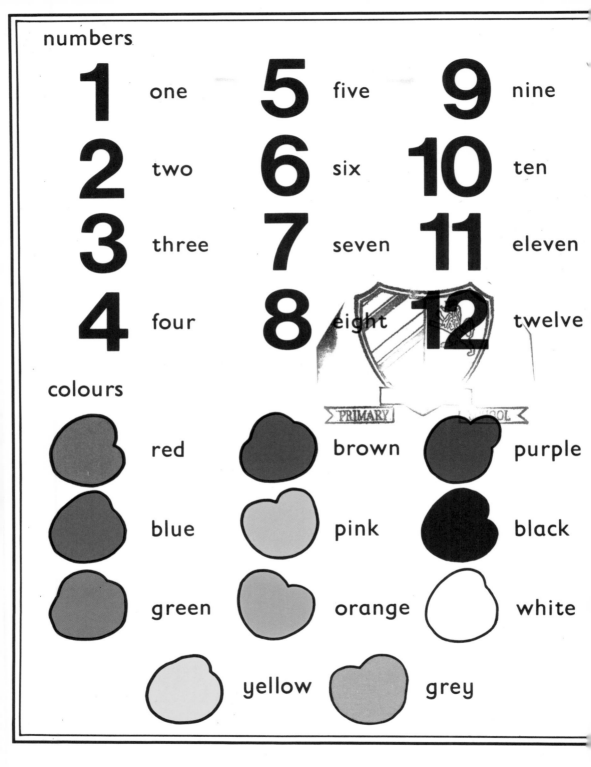

red	brown	purple
blue	pink	black
green	orange	white
	yellow	grey

Fran Kelly Ann Ranjit

bikes

1 How many bikes can you see?
2 Are all the bikes the same colour?
3 Is Kelly on a brown bike?
4 Can you ride a two wheel bike?
5 Is Ranjit on the blue bike?
6 How many wheels can you see?
7 Who is riding the red bike?
8 Are there more boys than girls on bikes?
9 Who is riding the blue bike?
10 How many adults are watching the children?
11 Are the riders wearing helmets?
12 Are the children riding on a track?

1 This camel has —
   legs and — hump.

2 This clock has —
   hands and — face.

3 This desk has —
   legs and — top.

4 This rabbit has —
   nose and — ears.

5 This robin has —
   legs and — wings.

canoes

1   Can you see more than one red canoe?
2   How many children are in canoes?
3   Is there a purple canoe on the bank?
4   Which canoe is upside down?
5   How many canoes are not being used?
6   Is there a boy in the green canoe?
7   What number is the yellow canoe?
8   Is there a girl in the orange canoe?
9   How many canoes are on the bank?
10   How many paddles can you see?
11   In which canoe are there two children?
12   Have you ever been in a canoe?

mice

fish

monkey

puppies

pet food

kittens

pet shop

1 What kind of shop is this?
2 Can you see six mice?
3 Are all the kittens awake?
4 How many tins of pet food can you see?
5 Which animal is by itself?
6 What colour are the fish?
7 How many puppies can you see?
8 Are the puppies bigger than the kittens?
9 Does this shop sell fish?
10 Are all the puppies the same colour?
11 Do mice have long tails?
12 Which of the pets would you like to buy?

yes or no

1 Can an egg crack?
2 Can a pin prick?
3 Has a needle got an eye?
4 Can a doll run?
5 Has a frog got wings?
6 Can a clock tick?
7 Can a brick swim?
8 Can a man wink?
9 Is a jelly hot?
10 Can a pig grunt?
11 Will a leg bend?
12 Can a house jump?

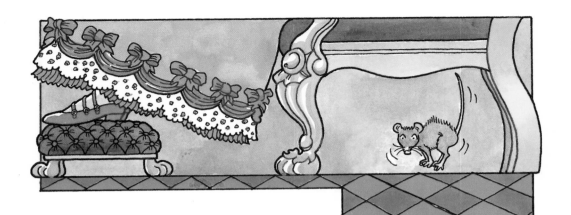

Pussy-Cat, Pussy-Cat
Where have you been?
I've been to London
To look at the queen.
Pussy-Cat, Pussy-Cat
What did you there?
I frightened a little mouse
Under her chair.

1 Is this poem about a dog?
2 Where had Pussy-Cat been?
3 Who did Pussy-Cat go to see in
   London?
4 Where was the mouse?
5 Did Pussy-Cat see the mouse?
6 Who was frightened?
7 Have you been to London?
8 Have you seen the queen?

canoe bike camel clock

1   You can ride on me.
    Your legs make me go.
    I have two wheels.
    I am a —.

2   I am long and thin.
    You sit in me.
    I go on water.
    I am a —.

3   I have two hands.
    I have one face.
    I tell the time.
    I am a —.

4   You can ride on me.
    I have four legs.
    I have a hump.
    I am a —.

astronaut

1 Can you see an astronaut?
2 Is the astronaut wearing a helmet?
3 What colour is the helmet?
4 Is the astronaut wearing boots?
5 Can you see the astronaut's hands?
6 Is the astronaut sitting down?
7 Can the astronaut sit down in his suit?
8 What colour is the astronaut's suit?
9 Can you see the astronaut's eyes?
10 Is the astronaut wearing a belt?

1 How many children can you see?
2 What lesson are they having?
3 How many boys are on the ropes?
4 What colour is the mat?
5 How many children are standing by the mat?
6 Can you jump over the box?
7 How many children are on the benches?
8 Does a boy or a girl have the hoop?
9 What colour are the balls?
10 Do you like P.E. lessons?
11 Do you think P.E. helps to keep you fit?
12 Which teacher takes you for P.E.?

on off

1   The big television set is —.

2   The little television set is —.

3   The big blue lamp is —.

4   The little blue lamp is —.

5   The big orange kettle is —.

6   The little orange kettle is —.

7   The big gas fire is —.

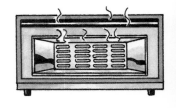

8   The little gas fire is —.

disco dancing

1 How many children can you see?
2 Are all the children dancing?
3 Can you do disco dancing?
4 How many children are sitting down?
5 Are all the boys dancing?
6 What colour is the disc jockey's shirt?
7 Is the disc jockey wearing a hat?
8 Do you think disco dancing is fun?
9 Do you think disco dancing keeps you fit?
10 Have you been to a disco?

cows

horses

farmer

sheep dog

sheep

hens

farmyard

1 How many hens can you see?
2 What colour are the hens?
3 Can you see more sheep than hens?
4 Are the sheep eating grass?
5 Which animals are black and white?
6 Are all the cows the same colours?
7 How many horses can you see?
8 Which animals are being fed by the farmer?
9 Are all the horses the same colour?
10 What kind of dog can you see?
11 Have you been to a farm?
12 Would you like to work on a farm?

1   How many children are in the sand-pit?
2   Do you like playing with sand?
3   What colour is the slide?
4   Do you think this is a big slide?
5   How many children are on the steps of the slide?
6   Are all the swings full?
7   Do you like the slide better than the swings?
8   Can you see a bucket and spade?
9   What colour are the swings?
10 How many boys are on the slide?

swings

sand-pit

slide

kangaroos

giraffe

lions

monkeys

elephants

bears

1   I can see five —.
2   I can see six —.
3   I can see four —.
4   I can see three —.
5   I can see one —.
6   I can see two —.

big dipper

1 What colour is the big dipper?
2 Is the big dipper going up or down?
3 Is the big dipper full?
4 Do the children on the big dipper look happy?
5 Does the big dipper go very fast?
6 Have you been on the big dipper?
7 How much is a ride on the big dipper?
8 Do you think a ride on the big dipper is fun?
9 Does the big dipper run on tracks?
10 Will it feel windy on the big dipper?
11 Do people scream when the big dipper goes up?
12 Which way is the big dipper going when people scream?

astronaut   television   big dipper   rabbit

1   You can ride on me.
I go up and down.
I go very fast.
I am the —.

2   I have a helmet.
I go in a rocket.
I go to the moon.
I am an —.

3   I can hop.
I have a fluffy tail.
I have long floppy ears.
I am a —.

4   You can switch me on and off.
You can see pictures on me.
I have a screen.
I am a —.

Thomas Nelson and Sons Ltd
Nelson House Mayfield Road
Walton-on-Thames Surrey
KT12 5PL UK

51 York Place
Edinburgh
EH1 3JD UK

Nelson Blackie
Westercleddens Road
Bishopsbriggs
Glasgow
G64 2NZ UK

Thomas Nelson (Hong Kong) Ltd
Toppan Building 10/F
22a Westlands Road
Quarry Bay Hong Kong

Thomas Nelson Australia
102 Dodds Street
South Melbourne
Victoria 3205 Australia

Nelson Canada
1120 Birchmount Road
Scarborough Ontario
M1K 5G4 Canada

© Constance Milburn 1984
Illustrated by David Brogan

First published by Blackie and Son Ltd 1984
ISBN 0-216-91651-8

This edition published by Thomas Nelson and Sons Ltd 1992

ISBN 0-17-422488-5
NPN 9 8 7 6 5 4 3